PLAIN SPEAKING 1

by Wendy Harris

Hong Kong
Oxford University Press

Oxford University Press

OXFORD NEW YORK TORONTO
DELHI BOMBAY CALCUTTA MADRAS KARACHI
PETALING JAYA SINGAPORE HONG KONG TOKYO
NAIROBI DAR ES SALAAM CAPE TOWN
MELBOURNE AUCKLAND
and associated companies in
BERLIN IBADAN

OXFORD is a trade mark of Oxford University Press

ISBN 0 19 581152 6

Cover design by George Kwan; Illustrations by Tom Briggs
Illustration on p.7 from *Realistic English Drills 1* by
Brian Abbs, Vivian Cook and Mary Underwood
© Oxford University Press

*Printed in Hong Kong by Nordica Printing Co.
Published by Oxford University Press, Warwick House, Hong Kong*

Preface

General aims

The material in this book is supplementary and is not intended to stand alone as a course, although it does follow the approved Syllabus for Secondary Schools.

The objective is to present structural elements of the English language which the students have already met, in natural situations.

To achieve fluent conversational English, students should speak as much as possible during classes. This is often difficult because of lack of time. Choral drilling is useful to familiarize the whole class with the main structures, vocabulary items and idiomatic phrases in each unit, but as soon as the teacher feels that the students can manipulate these essentials, he should encourage small group or pair work to give each child the maximum opportunity to speak. Stronger students can work with weaker ones to help out while the teacher moves around monitoring groups and dealing with any difficulties that occur.

Unit breakdown

Each of the twenty units in this book is divided into four sections. The first section, *Dialogue*, consists of a short illustrated Situation paragraph which sets the scene for the dialogue itself. The short questions are to make sure that the situation has been fully understood. The dialogue comes next.

The second section, *Pronunciation*, deals with sound production, intonation or stress. Generally speaking, only one of these three is emphasized in each unit, but the others should not be completely ignored. If two contrasting vowel sounds are being taught, the teacher should make sure that when the students practise these sounds in the context of words and sentences, their stress and intonation patterns are acceptable.

The last two sections, *Language Practice 1 and 2*, highlight the main structural points in the dialogue and offer further practice of these in different situations. Teachers will notice that Language Practice 1 is generally more controlled than Language Practice 2. This is to ensure that the students have adequately consolidated the structures and will be comfortable when they try to manipulate them in freer conversational situations.

Suggestions for presentation and use of each section

1   *Situation*   Either as a short reading comprehension or aural comprehension. The illustration can provide the basis for general questions and 'scene setting' before the students read or hear the text. After presenting the text, the teacher can then check that the Situation has been fully understood by using the Questions orally round the class. More questions can be added if the teacher feels particular vocabulary items are unfamiliar to the students. If the teacher decides to present the Situation orally, it is suggested that he allow the students to read the text silently after the Questions have been completed. Understanding the Situation is essential for the effective use of the dialogue which follows.

2   *Dialogue*   If the Dialogue is presented as an aural comprehension exercise on tape, the procedure might be as follows:

- Pre-teach necessary vocabulary items.
- Teacher plays tape all through while students look at the picture, *not* the text.
- Teacher asks check questions to make sure the students have the gist of the conversation.
- Teacher plays tape section by section — perhaps three or four lines at a time, breaking at an appropriate point — and asks more detailed check questions. Students should still *not* see the text.
- Teacher then plays tape line by line or sentence by sentence, and asks the class chorally and/or individually to repeat each section, copying the intonation and pronunciation.
- Teacher plays tape once more while students follow text in their books.
- Teacher allows students to read text silently in their own time and ask any questions they need to.

If a tape is *not* used, the teacher may read the Dialogue himself or assign two students to read it after having prepared it for a homework exercise. After the Dialogue has been presented and the teacher is sure the students have fully understood it, the class can be divided into groups or pairs to practise by themselves. After a few minutes, the teacher might reproduce a skeleton dialogue on the board using only key words from the text. The students should close their books and try to re-create the Dialogue using the skeleton. A final rounding off exercise which is always fun and tends to stick in the students' minds is *acting out*. The teacher may choose one or two couples to re-arrange the furniture at the front of the class and then act out the scene with movements, appropriate gestures and facial expressions. Non-acting students can be involved as stage managers, directors, prompts (usually essential!) etc. This free stage activity is particularly valuable if the students can be encouraged to criticise each other's performances constructively and, needless to say, in English. At lower levels the teacher will have to be instrumental in this criticism by asking simple *yes/no* questions like 'Can you hear him?' 'Is he speaking slowly?' 'Is that right?'.

3   *Pronunciation*   The elements of pronunciation, stress and intonation which are covered in this section of each unit are all based on problems likely to arise from the Dialogue. The pronunciation point may be related to the structure, particular vocabulary items or the way words are linked together in connected speech. Examples are given from the Dialogue and/or Language Practice sections so that the teacher can refer back and give the exercise a meaningful context. Pairs practice is used frequently, both for the production of individual sounds and the formation of intonation patterns. It is suggested that, once the teacher has given two or three examples and drilled them thoroughly with the whole class, he should then divide the students into groups or pairs and let them practise at their own speed. Once the idea of self-help has been established, students will be eager to check their partners and will become much more able to spot mistakes in their own oral production. It is unreasonable to expect perfect pronunciation from anyone but a native speaker so teachers should not set their sights too high. They should insist on clarity and make sure that the students are comprehensible both to the teacher and each other. The Pronunciation section should take the least classroom time of all the sections.

4   *Language practice*   The idea of these sections is to give the students plenty of manipulation of the structures which occur in the Dialogue. Again choral drilling for one or two examples will give the students a solid base. They can then practise together in groups or pairs, concentrating on accuracy, speed and good pronunciation. During lesson preparation, teachers might find it helpful to collect together some extra material appropriate to the particular unit, such as maps, flashcards, etc. This material can be introduced as an exten-

sion of the Language Practice exercises and form the basis for free-stage work once the teacher is sure that the students are able to cope adequately with the structures. The real test comes in free-stage work when students are encouraged to make up their own situations and dialogues. It quickly becomes apparent whether they have grasped the concept of the structure and are able to manipulate it comfortably or not.

Social register and idiom

The English language is not just a collection of words governed by complicated rules. It is a means of communication which also enables its speakers to express emotions and delicate shades of meaning. People decide how to behave towards each other in any social situation not so much by what they say but how they say it. The word 'yes' can express anger, impatience, joy, surprise, horror and many more emotions, simply by a change in the pitch and intonation of the speaker's voice.

Similarly, attitudes towards people, situations and ideas can be made very clear by the use of simple idioms. Without these idioms, the language sounds stilted and 'bookish'. It lacks a natural flow and warmth. Teachers will find idioms in some of the units in this book, phrases like 'what a mess' and 'what on earth's the matter?'. Students should be made aware that these idioms cannot be translated or understood word by word. They must be taken as a unit, treated, if you like, as one word. They can most effectively be presented to the students through simple situations.

At lower levels it is often useful to treat isolated examples of more complex grammatical structures as idioms. The students need to know what they mean and why they are used in one particular context, but they do not need, at this stage, to be able to manipulate the structure and use it elsewhere. An example of this idiomatic treatment of structure occurs in Unit One where Paul says 'I keep getting lost'. All the students need to know about this fairly advanced structure at this stage is that it means that Paul doesn't know where to go or where anything is because he is new to the school. The students do not need to be able to make negative, question and other forms using 'keep' with the 'ing' form of the verb.

Social register means being able to select the appropriate group of words from a selection of phrases or sentences which all basically mean the same thing. 'Shut the door!' 'I wonder if you'd mind shutting the door, please,' and 'It's rather chilly in here, isn't it?' all mean 'I am cold and I want you to shut the door'. Which one you chose would depend on whom you were talking to and where you were. An example of social register which occurs in this book is the use of 'Mum' versus 'mother'. Children tend to address their parents familiarly as 'Mum' and 'Dad' but when they are talking to other people about them will refer to them as 'mother' and 'father'. Social register, like idiom, is another means of establishing relationships with people and attitudes towards things. It gives colour, warmth and above all fluency to the language. It is a very necessary part of English, which would sound rather like a talking computer without it.

PHONETIC SYMBOLS USED IN THE TEXT

vowels

/ɪ/	as in	s*i*t
/i/	as in	s*ea*t
/ə/	as in	*a*bove
/æ/	as in	c*a*t
/ɑ/	as in	p*ar*t
/ɜ/	as in	w*or*k
/ɔ/	as in	d*oo*r

Consonants

/ð/	as in	*th*is
/f/	as in	*f*at
/v/	as in	*v*alley
/s/	as in	*s*ix
/θ/	as in	*th*in
/w/	as in	*w*eek
/k/	as in	*c*at
/t/	as in	*t*en
/d/	as in	*d*og
/g/	as in	*g*irl
/l/	as in	*l*ife
/r/	as in	*r*ed
/z/	as in	goe*s*
/h/	as in	*h*old

Contents

Present simple of 'to be' • this/that/these/those • What's this/that? •
's a • What are these/those? • They are

Present simple for nationalities and occupations • 'can' for skills

Present simple of 'to be' • adjectives for describing people

What do you like? • I like + noun object • I like + gerund object •
some/any + countable and uncountable nouns

my/your/his/her • belong to • Adjectives for describing objects

Greetings and introductions • Where do you live?

had better do • Prepositions of place

Asking for and giving the time

Telling the time • Vocabulary for discussing entertainment

How are you? • Asking for and giving directions • Imperative •
Prepositions of place and movement

Asking for and giving directions

Present continuous for action now • Verbs with 'get' • had better do

Anaphoric one/ones • 'going to' for anticipated action in the near future

Present continuous in contact clauses • 'going to' for anticipated action
in the near future

'have got' for discussing illnesses • Past simple with adverbial time phrases

will' for requests • 'shall' for offers

ever' and 'never' with present simple • adverbial time phrases

Present simple with adverbs of frequency • Present simple contrasted
with past simple

Past simple

Present perfect • Present perfect contrasted with past simple

1 Paul's First Day

Dialogue

Situation

It's Monday. It's the first day of term. David's in the playground. He's talking to Paul. Paul's a new student. Today's his first day. He's nervous. David's friendly and helpful. He's helping Paul to settle in.

Questions

1 Is it Saturday?
2 What day of the week is it?
3 Is it the first day of term?
4 Is David in the classroom?
5 Where's David?
6 Is Paul there too?
7 Is Paul a new student?
8 How's he feeling?
9 Is David friendly?
10 What's David doing?

Handwritten answers:
(1) No, it isn't.
(2) Monday.
(3) Yes, it is.
(4) No, he isn't.
(5) He's in the play-ground.
(6) No, he isn't.
(7) Yes, he is.
(8) He's nervous (9) Yes, he is
(10) He's helping Paul to settle in.

Dialogue

David: Hello. Are you new?
Paul: Yes. Today's my first day.
David: What's your name?
Paul: It's Paul Ho. What's yours?
David: David Tsui. Are you a Form One student?
Paul: Yes. Are you?
David: No. I'm in Form Two. Which class are you in?
Paul: 1C. My teacher's Miss Lam.
David: Do you know your way round?
Paul: Not yet. I keep getting lost.
David: I'll show you round. There's plenty of time before the next class.
Paul: Thanks.

Here are some of David's questions. Practise saying them aloud and make your voice rise at the end of each question.

Are you new?

Are you a Form One student?

Do you know your way round?

Now look at these pictures. Make *is* or *are* questions about each picture. Here are two examples:

Picture 1   Is he tall?   Picture 5   Is she tall?

        Yes, he is.   No, she isn't. She's short.

Remember, the question goes *up* and the answer goes *down*.
Now make two questions about each picture.

tall   young   fat   poor

short   old   thin   rich

Language Practice 1

This is Paul's satchel. These are some of the things inside it.

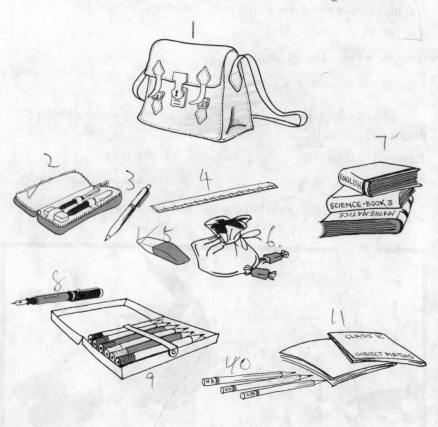

Point to the different things and ask your partner questions like this:

What's this?
It's a pencil case.

What are these?
They're crayons.

What's that?
It's a rubber.

What are those?
They're pencils.

1. What's this?
   It's a school-bag.
2. What's that?
   It's a pen
3. What's this?
   It's a ruler
4. What're these?
   They're sweets.
5. What're these?
   They're books.
6. What's that?
   They's kinpen
7. What're thing?
   They's oxsige books.

This is a floor plan of David's school.

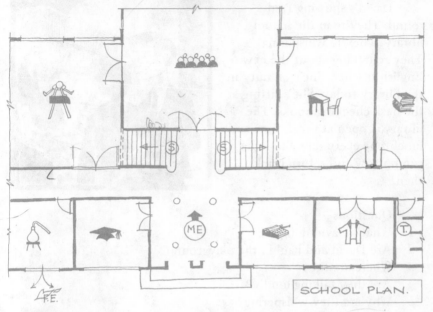

SCHOOL PLAN.

This is the key:

(ME)	main entrance	👕	cloakroom	📖	classroom
(S)	stairs	📇	school office	📚	library
(T)	toilets	🎓	staffroom	👥	school hall
F.E.	fire escape	⚗	science laboratory	🤸	gymnasium

Ask your partner what the different symbols stand for. Make questions and answers like this:

What does this stand for?   What does that stand for?
It stands for 'main entrance'.   It stands for 'classroom'.

Now look at the floor plan again. Imagine you are showing your partner round the school. Your partner will ask you questions about the different parts of the school and you will give him the answers, like this:

What's this?   What's that?
It's the main entrance.   It's a classroom.

Is that the gymnasium?   Is this the staffroom?
No, it isn't. It's the school hall.   Yes, it is.

2 The New Teacher

Situation

David's showing Paul round. They're in the school library. They're whispering. They're talking about the new English teacher. She's on duty in the library today. She's sitting at the desk checking books. The library is open at break-time and lunchtime every day. Students can borrow and return books then.

Questions

1 What's David doing? *He showing Paul round.*
2 Are David and Paul in the playground? *No, they aren't.*
3 Where are they? *They are in the library.*
4 Are they talking loudly? *No, they aren't.*
5 Why are they whispering? *Beause they in the library.*
6 Are they talking about the new English teacher? *Yes, they are.*
7 Is she on duty in the library today? *Yes, she is.*
8 Where's she sitting? *She's sitting at the desk check...*
9 Is the library open every day? *Yes, it is.*
10 Can students borrow and return books every day? *Yes, they can. books*

Dialogue

Paul: Who's that over there?
David: That's the new teacher.
Paul: Is she Chinese?
David: No, she comes from England.
Paul: What does she teach?
David: English, of course.
Paul: Is she your teacher?
David: Yes. She teaches my class three times a week.
Paul: Can she speak Chinese?
David: Not very much.
Paul: It's a good thing you can speak English!

Intonation Practice

Here are some questions about the new teacher. Practise saying them aloud and make your voice fall at the end of each question.

Who's that?

What does she teach?

Where does she come from?

Now look at the map and make some more *Wh* questions. Remember, *Wh* questions go *down*. Here are some examples:

Where does he come from?

He comes from France.

What's his nationality?

He's French.

Where do they come from?

They come from Britain.

What's their nationality?

They're British.

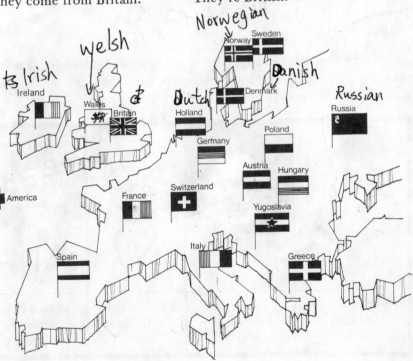

7

Language Practice 1

This is Studio 2 at RTV. Richard Dean is a television interviewer. He's making a programme about foreigners in Hong Kong. He's asking his guests about their nationalities and their occupations. Here's the first interview.

Dean: Good evening. Welcome to our programme.
Dupont: Thank you. Good evening, Mr. Dean.
Dean: Would you tell us your name, please?
Dupont: I'm Paul Dupont.
Dean: Where do you come from, Mr. Dupont?
Dupont: I come from France.
Dean: What do you do, Mr. Dupont?
Dupont: I'm a chef.
Dean: Thank you, Mr. Dupont.

There are four more guests on the programme tonight. Imagine you are Richard Dean. Interview each guest and ask about their nationalities and occupations.

Anna Schmidt	James Walker	Patricia Green	Manuel Plata
Germany	America	Britain	Spain
singer	lawyer	doctor	bullfighter

Here are some questions you can use:

What do you do?   Where do you come from?
What's your job?   What's your nationality?

Language Practice 2

Do you remember this question?

Paul: Can she speak Chinese?
David: Not very much.

Paul and David are talking about their new English teacher. Here are some more questions about her. Study the answers carefully.

Paul: Can she read Chinese?
David: No. Not at all.

Paul: Can she speak English?
David: Yes. Very well indeed.

Paul: Can she ride a bicycle?
David: Not very well.

Now look at these pictures and make *Can* questions and answers with your partner.

swim/very well indeed	cook/not very well	drive/very well indeed	ride/not at all
speak French/ not very well	play/very well indeed	add/not at all	type/not very well

9

3 David Falls in Love

Dialogue

Situation

It's half past five. David's at home. He's in the kitchen. He's talking to his mother. She's asking him about the new English teacher. David thinks she's very beautiful. He's got a crush on her. He stayed behind after school to talk to her. That's why he's late home. Now he's sitting at the kitchen table dreaming about her.

Questions

1 Is David at school? *No, he isn't*
2 Where is he? *He's at home.*
3 What's the time? *It's half past five.*
4 Is David home early? *No, he isn't*
5 Why not? *He stayed behind after school to*
6 What's Mrs. Tsui asking him about? *She's asking him about to new*
7 Does David think the new teacher's beautiful? *Yes, he does. tea*
8 Is he in love with her? *Yes, he is.*
9 Who's he dreaming about? *The new English teacher.*

Dialogue

Mrs. Tsui:	You're home late today, David. How was school?
David:	Not bad. There's a new English teacher.
Mrs. Tsui:	Oh? What's she like?
David:	She's beautiful!
Mrs. Tsui:	Is she old or young?
David:	She's quite young and her hair's blond.
Mrs. Tsui:	Is she strict?
David:	Not really. Her eyes are blue.
Mrs. Tsui:	Can she speak Chinese?
David:	Not much. She's very tall and slim.
Mrs. Tsui:	David! Stop dreaming! It's time to do your homework.
David:	Oh, all right. I think English is my favourite subject.

Intonation Practice

Do you remember Mrs. Tsui's question about the new English teacher? Here it is again:

Mrs. Tsui: Is she old or young?

Notice the intonation pattern goes *up* and then *down*. Here are some more questions about the new English teacher. Practise the intonation pattern carefully.

Is she English or Chinese?

Is she plump or slim?

Is she tall or short?

Is she strict or easy-going?

Here is a description of Jane Tsui. How many *or* questions can you make from the description.

Jane's older than her brother. She's not in Form Two, she's in Form Three. She's tall for her age and she's rather plump. She's clever at school work but she's lazy at sports. She's also rather untidy at home. She's quite pretty and very friendly. Her friends all think she's very good-natured and generous.

Now practise these *or* questions with your partner. Make your voice go *up* and then *down*. Make sure your partner gives you the right answer.

1　Is Jane older or younger than her brother?
2　Is she in Form Two or Form Three?
3　Is she tall or short?
4　Is she plump or slim?
5　Is she good or bad at school work?
6　Is she good or bad at sports?
7　Is she tidy or untidy at home?
8　Is she pretty or ugly?
9　Is she friendly or unfriendly?

Language Practice 1

Here's David's new English teacher. Can you complete these questions and answers about her?

What colour .*are*. her eyes?
They. are blue.

What colour .*is*. hair?
.*Its*. blond.

How tall .*is*. she?
She. is very tall.

How old .*is*. she?
She. is quite young.

Here's David with George, the family pet. Ask and answer questions about both of them.

ears?   eyes?
fur?   hair?
big?   tall?
old?   old?

12

Here is some information about the people who appeared on Richard Dean's television programme. Can you describe each person from the information?

Name	Anna Schmidt	James Walker	Patricia Green	Manuel Plata
Age	34	52	40	28
Nationality	German	American	British	Spanish
Occupation	Singer	Lawyer	Doctor	Bullfighter
Height	5'2"	6'3"	5'6"	5'4"
Weight	150 lbs	220 lbs	120 lbs	115 lbs
Hair	red	brown	blond	black
Eyes	green	brown	blue	brown

Now you know how to describe what someone looks like. Can you describe someone's character? Here are some character adjectives and some pictures of people.

bad-tempered   mean   shy   good-natured   generous
friendly

good-natured   shy   friendly

mean   generous   bad-tempered

13

4 Starving to Death

Dialogue

Situation

Jane has just got home. She's very hungry. She's very thirsty too. She wants a snack. She likes potato crisps and bananas but there aren't any. She likes orange juice but there isn't any. Mrs. Tsui's offering her some peanuts and some milk. Jane doesn't like peanuts or milk. She's so hungry because she left her lunchbox on the bus this morning. She didn't have any lunch.

Questions

1 Has Jane just got home? *Yes*
2 Is she hungry? *Yes,*
3 Is she thirsty? *Yes,*
4 What does Jane want?
5 Does she like potato crisps? *Yes*
6 Are there any? *No*
7 Does she like orange juice? *Yes*
8 Is there any? *No*
9 Did she have any lunch? *No*

Dialogue

Jane: Are there any biscuits? I'm starving.

Mrs. Tsui: Just a minute. I'll have a look in the packet. No, there aren't any.

Jane: Are there any potato crisps, then?

Mrs. Tsui: No, there aren't, but there are some peanuts.

Jane: Oh Mum, you know I don't like peanuts.

Mrs. Tsui: Well, have an apple.

Jane: I'd rather have a banana. Are there any bananas?

Mrs. Tsui: No, there aren't. David had the last one.

Jane: Is there any orange juice? I'm thirsty too.

Mrs. Tsui: No. There aren't any biscuits or potato crisps. There aren't any bananas and there isn't any orange juice. Here's a glass of milk. Why are you so hungry anyway?

Jane: I left my lunchbox on the bus this morning. I haven't had anything to eat all day.

Pronunciation Practice

/ð/

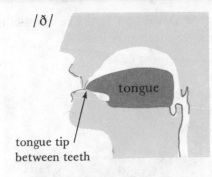

tongue

tongue tip
between teeth

This sound is rather difficult. Put the tip of your tongue between your teeth and practise saying these words aloud:

this	those
that	then
these	there

Here's the beginning of the dialogue again. Practise saying it with your partner.

Jane: Are there any biscuits? I'm starving.

Mrs. Tsui: Just a minute. I'll have a look in the packet. No, there aren't any.

Now look at these pictures and make more conversations. The parts in colour are the parts you can change.

cakes/tin   milk/carton   fruit/bowl   ice-cream/fridge

crisps/packet   sweets/cupboard   tea/teapot   orange juice/bottle

15

Language Practice 1

Here are some of the things that David and Jane like and some of the things they hate. Can you answer these questions?

What does Jane like to eat?
What does Jane like to drink?
What TV programmes does Jane like to watch?
What music does Jane like to listen to?
What subjects does Jane like to study?

	Jane likes	Jane hates	David likes	David hates
Food	potato crisps bananas	peanuts apples	peanuts cakes	oranges pears
Drink	orange juice Coca Cola	milk coffee	Coca Cola tea	orange juice coffee
TV	cartoons horror films	Westerns news	Westerns cartoons	Hawaii Five O horror films
Music	Beatles Cat Stevens	Rolling Stones Cliff Richard	Rolling Stones Beatles	Supremes Cat Stevens
School	History Art	English Science	English Maths	Art History

Now ask the same kind of questions about David. Then ask your partner what he or she likes.

Look at the lists of things that David and Jane like and hate. Make questions and answers about them with your partner like this:

Does Jane like potato crisps?
Yes, she does.

Does Jane like peanuts?
No, she doesn't, but David does.

Does David like them too?
I don't know.

Does Jane like the Beatles?
Yes, she does, and so does David.

How many different questions and answers can you make from the lists?

Language Practice 2

Mr. and Mrs. Tsui are at a restaurant. They're looking at the menu. They're trying to decide what to have.

Mrs. Tsui:	Have some soup.
Mr. Tsui:	Is there any tomato soup?
Mrs. Tsui:	Yes, there is.
Mr. Tsui:	Good. I'll have some tomato soup, please.
Waiter:	What will you have to follow, Sir?
Mrs. Tsui:	Have a pork chop.
Mr. Tsui:	I don't like pork chops very much. I'd rather have a lamb chop.
Waiter:	Some tomato soup and a lamb chop. Very good, Sir.

Here's the menu.

Menu

SOUP —
CREAM of CHICKEN
CREAM of TOMATO
CREAM of MUSHROOM

MEAT —
LAMB CHOPS
PORK CHOPS
FILLET STEAK
CHICKEN LEGS

FISH —
MACAU SOLE
FILLET of GAROUPA

VEGETABLES —
POTATOES
CARROTS
PEAS
GREEN BEANS

DESSERTS —
FRESH LYCHEES
PEACHES
PEARS
MANGOES

Practise this conversation with your partner and then try to make up some different ones.

Mrs. Tsui:	. . . . . a chop.
Mr. Tsui:	. . . . . lamb chops?
Mrs. Tsui:	Yes, ... are.
Mr. Tsui:	Good. I'll . . . . ., please.
Waiter:	What . . . . . for dessert, Sir?
Mrs. Tsui:	. . . . . some peaches.
Mr. Tsui:	I . . . . . very much. I'd . . . . . some lychees.
Waiter:	. . . . . lamb chop and . . . . . lychees. Very good, Sir.

17

5 What a Mess!

Dialogue

Situation

Mrs. Tsui's very angry today. Jane and David share a bedroom. Jane's very untidy. The bedroom's in a terrible mess. Jane's shoes are on the floor. Her T-shirt's on the bed. Her tennis racket's under the bed. David's clothes are all over the place too. Mrs. Tsui wants the children to tidy everything up.

Questions

1 Is Mrs. Tsui in a good mood today?
2 Do Jane and David share a bedroom?
3 Is Jane tidy?
4 Is the bedroom tidy?
5 How does the bedroom look?
6 Where are Jane's shoes?
7 Where's her T-shirt?
8 Is David's tennis racket under the bed?
9 Are David's clothes in the wardrobe?
10 What does Mrs. Tsui want the children to do?

Dialogue

Mrs. Tsui: Your bedroom's in a terrible mess!
David: It's not my fault. Jane's so untidy.
Jane: That's not fair. I'm not untidy!
Mrs. Tsui: Stop arguing, both of you, and tidy everything up.
David: Oh, all right. Are these your shoes?
Jane: Yes, they are. Put them in the cupboard, please.
David: Is this your T-shirt?
Jane: No, that's mine, on the bed.
David: Hey! That's my tennis racket!
Jane: No it isn't. It's mine.
David: Well, where's mine, then?
Jane: I don't know.

18

Stress and Pronunciation Practice

Stressed words are very important. You can change the meaning of a sentence by changing the stressed word. Practise saying these two lines from the dialogue with your partner. Make sure you put the stressed words in the right places.

David: Is this your T-shirt?

Jane: No, that's mine, on the bed.

Now look at these pictures and make more questions and answers. Be careful with the stress.

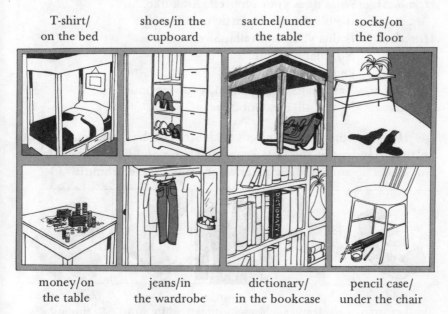

| T-shirt/ on the bed | shoes/in the cupboard | satchel/under the table | socks/on the floor |
| money/on the table | jeans/in the wardrobe | dictionary/ in the bookcase | pencil case/ under the chair |

Sometimes we can use stress to disagree with people. Practise saying these lines from the dialogue with your partner.

David: That's my tennis racket.

Jane: No it isn't. It's mine.

Now point to each picture below and practise disagreeing with your partner. Make your stressed words strong and clear.

Mr. Tsui is rather forgetful. He often loses things. When he loses something, he goes to the Lost Property Office.

Attendant:	Good morning, Sir. Can I help you?
Mr. Tsui:	Yes. I've lost my umbrella.
Attendant:	What does your umbrella look like, Sir?
Mr. Tsui:	It's black with a plastic handle.
Attendant:	Is this your umbrella, Sir?
Mr. Tsui:	No, that isn't mine.
Attendant:	Perhaps this is yours?
Mr. Tsui:	Yes, that's mine. Thank you very much.
Attendant:	Not at all, Sir. Goodbye.

Here are some more things which Mr. Tsui has lost. Imagine you are the attendant at the Lost Property Office and your partner is Mr. Tsui. Make up some more conversations using these prompts.

gold/ leather strap	grey/ red feather	brown/ black buttons	red wool/ white strips	black leather/ fur lining

Here are some more situations:

1 This is your car. It's been stolen. Make up a conversation with the policeman at your local police station. Begin like this:

Policeman:	Good morning, Sir/Madam. Can I help you?
Mr./Mrs. . . :	Yes. My car's been stolen.

2 This is your dog. You've lost it. Make up a conversation with the policeman at your local police station. Begin like this:

Policeman:	Good morning, Sir/Madam. Can I help you?
Mr./Mrs. . . :	Yes. I've lost my dog.

Language Practice 2

WHO DO THESE THINGS BELONG TO?

Charlie	Peter	Nancy
chef	policeman	nurse

recipe book

handcuffs

pair of shoes

boots

bandages

wooden spoon

uniform

thermometer

hat

6 Making Friends

Situation

David and Paul are good friends now. The Tsui family lives in Stanley. Paul doesn't live in Stanley. He lives on Kowloon side. David has invited Paul to come to Stanley and meet his parents and his sister. He's introducing Paul to everyone. It's almost supper-time. It's a long journey back to Kowloon so Mrs. Tsui's inviting Paul to stay for supper.

Questions

1   Are David and Paul good friends?
2   Does the Tsui family live on Kowloon side?
3   Where does the Tsui family live?
4   Does Paul live there too?
5   Where does Paul live?
6   Are Paul and David at Paul's house?
7   Who is David introducing Paul to?
8   Is it supper-time?
9   Is Paul going to have supper with the Tsuis?
10   Why?

Dialogue

Mrs. Tsui: Is that you, David?
David: Yes, Mum. I'm home. I've brought one of my friends.
Mrs. Tsui: Bring him in. Let's meet him.
David: Come and meet my family. Mum, this is Paul Ho.
Mrs. Tsui: Hello, Paul. Come in.
Paul: How do you do, Mrs. Tsui. Thank you.
David: And this is my sister, Jane. Jane, this is Paul.
Paul: Hello, Jane.
Jane: Hello, Paul. Do you live near here?
Paul: No. I live in Kowloon.
Jane: Whereabouts in Kowloon?
Paul: In Tsim Sha Tsui, near the Police Station.
Mrs. Tsui: That's a long way away. You'd better stay for supper.
Paul: Thank you very much, Mrs. Tsui.

22

/f/ /v/

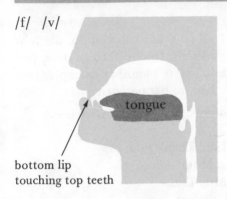

tongue

bottom lip
touching top teeth

/f/ is a voiceless sound. /v/ is a voiced sound. They are both made in the same way. Practise these pairs of words:

/f/	/v/
ferry	very
fan	van
fault	vault
few	view
feel	veal
fast	vast

Hold the palm of your hand in front of your month. Say /f/. You can feel the breath on your hand. Now say /v/. You can feel very little breath.

Point to these pictures and say what they are. Is the first sound voiced or voiceless? Practise with your partner.

Language Practice 1

INTRODUCTIONS

In the dialogue for this unit, Paul says 'how do you do' when he is introduced to Mrs. Tsui. When you are introduced to an older person, it is polite to say 'how do you do'. Here's another example. Jane is introducing her best friend, Alice Lee, to her parents.

Jane:	Come and meet my parents. Dad, this is Alice Lee.
Mr. Tsui:	Hello, Alice, Come in.
Alice:	How do you do, Mr. Tsui. Thank you.
Jane:	And this is my mother. Mum, Alice.
Alice:	Pleased to meet you, Mrs. Tsui.

Now, imagine you are Jane. Introduce your classmate, Sally Yu, to your parents.

Jane:	Come . . . . . parents. Dad, ... Sally Yu.
Mr. Tsui:	. . . . ., Sally. . . . . . in.
Sally:	How . . . . . do, Mr. Tsui. Thank you.
Jane:	And . . . . . mother. Mum, Sally.
Mrs. Tsui:	. . . . ., Sally.
Sally:	Pleased . . . . ., Mrs. Tsui.

Now make up a complete conversation for yourself. You are David Tsui. You are introducing your classmate, James Leung, to your parents.

Language Practice 2

WHERE DO YOU LIVE?

Here are some questions you can ask your partner and the other people in your class. Look at the questions and answers carefully and then make your own conversations.

1 *Asking about the general area.*

Which side of the harbour do you live on?

I live	on	Hong Kong side.
	on	Kowloon side.
	in	the New Territories.

2 *Asking about the district.*

Whereabouts	on	Hong Kong side?		In	Central.
	on	Kowloon side?			Tsim Sha Tsui.
	in	the New Territories?			Shek Kong.

3 *Asking about the kind of building.*

Do you live	on an estate?
	in a block of flats?
	in a house?

4 *Asking for precise information.*

What's your address?   It's 18, Mody Road, Tsim Sha Tsui, Kowloon.

Which floor do you live on?   The third floor.

Here's David Tsui's address:

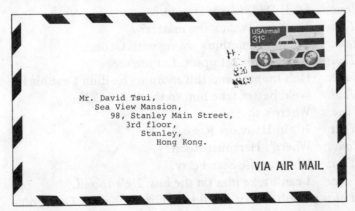

```
Mr. David Tsui,
   Sea View Mansion,
      98, Stanley Main Street,
         3rd floor,
            Stanley,
               Hong Kong.
```

USAirmail 31¢

VIA AIR MAIL

25

7 Something Wrong with George

Dialogue

Situation

David and Jane have a pet dog. He's called George. It's Saturday afternoon and David's playing football at Aberdeen. Jane's at home. Mr. Tsui's at home too. He's mending the tap in the kitchen. Jane's very worried because George isn't well. There's something wrong with one of his legs. He's not eating anything either. Jane doesn't know what to do but Mr. Tsui offers some good advice. He thinks they should take George to the R.S.P.C.A.

Questions

1 Have David and Jane got any pets?
2 Have they got a cat?
3 What kind of pet have they got?
4 What's his name?
5 Is Mr. Tsui at work today?
6 What's he doing?
7 Why isn't Jane happy?
8 Can George walk properly?
9 Where does Mr. Tsui think they should take him?

Dialogue

Jane: Dad! Dad, where are you?

Mr. Tsui: I'm here. What's the matter?

Jane: There's something wrong with George.

Mr. Tsui: Now, don't get upset. Let me see.

Jane: He's limping and this morning he didn't eat his food.

Mr. Tsui: We'd better take him to the R.S.P.C.A.

Jane: Where's that?

Mr. Tsui: It's in Harcourt Road.

Jane: Where's Harcourt Road?

Mr. Tsui: It's near the Star Ferry.

Jane: I can't take him on the bus. He's too ill.

Mr. Tsui: Don't worry. We'll take him in the car. Come on.

Pronunciation Practice

Some vowel sounds are *long* and some are *short*. Here are two lists of words. They sound exactly the same except for the vowel sound. The first list has a long /i/ sound and the second has a short /ɪ/ sound. Practise saying them aloud.

/i/	/ɪ/
seat	sit
heat	hit
beat	bit
eat	it
feet	fit
lead	lid
we'll	will

Ask your partner to close his book. Read words from each list to him. Ask him to tell you if the word you read comes from column 1 or column 2. Keep changing from one to the other to make it more difficult.

Here are some sentences where only one word changes. Sometimes the sound is /i/ and sometimes it's /ɪ/. Tell your partner to cover the left hand column. Read him a sentence from the left hand column and see if he can give you the right answer from the right hand column.

Look! There's a ship.	It's sinking.
Look! There's a sheep.	It's eating grass.
That boy beat me.	Yes, he won the race.
That boy bit me.	You're bleeding.
Where's the lead?	It's hanging on the hook.
Where's the lid.	It's on the saucepan.
Fill the cup.	It's full.
Feel the cup.	It's hot.

27

Language Practice 1

Jane is very upset in this unit because the family dog, George, isn't well. She doesn't know what to do about it, but her father offers some good advice. He says:

Mr. Tsui: We'd better take him to the R.S.P.C.A.

'Had better' is a friendly way to offer advice. When we use 'had better' in conversation, we usually shorten it to ''d better'. This is why Mr. Tsui says 'we'd better'. The long form is 'we had better'. Short forms are called contractions. Read these sentences about the Tsui family to your partner and ask him to offer advice. Make sure that he uses a contraction. Here's an example:

Mr. Tsui's lost his umbrella. (Lost Property Office)
He'd better go to the Lost Property Office.

Now you do the same.

1   David's got toothache. (dentist)
2   Jane's feeling ill. (doctor)
3   Mrs. Tsui needs some stamps. (post office)
4   Mr. Tsui hasn't got any money. (bank)
5   Somebody's stolen Mr. Tsui's car. (police station)

Sometimes we have to advise people *not* to do things. The last time that Mr. Tsui went to his doctor, the doctor advised him *not* to do several things. Here's an example:

Doctor: You're working too hard, Mr. Tsui. You'd better not work so hard.

Notice that in the first sentence he says 'too' and in the second he says 'so'. What else did the doctor advise Mr. Tsui *not* to do?

1   You're smoking too much.
2   You're eating too much.
3   You're drinking too much.
4   You're going to bed too late.
5   You're worrying too much.

Language Practice 2

Here are some useful prepositions:

next to   near   in   between   opposite

Now, using this street map of Happy Valley and these prepositions, ask questions about the different places marked on the map. Like this:

Where's the Hong Kong Football Club?
It's in Sports Road.
Where's Sports Road?
It's near the race course.

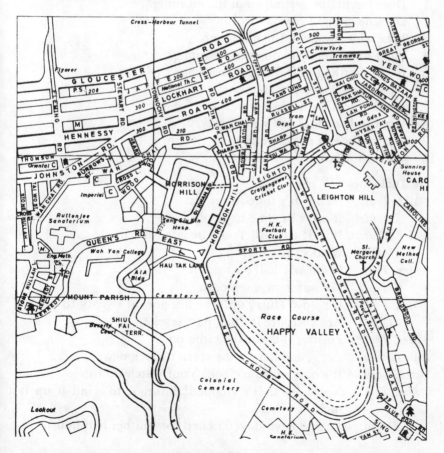

8 Too Early or too Late?

Situation

David hates getting up in the morning. He always gets up at the last minute. Mrs. Tsui shouts at him every morning because he's so sleepy. This morning, Mrs. Tsui's shouting as usual. Her watch says nearly half past seven. The bus leaves at twenty to eight and David's still in bed. David's watch says ten past seven. Neither is right. The seven o'clock news is just starting on the radio.

Questions

1. Does David like getting up in the morning?
2. Does he get up early?
3. Is he wide awake in the morning?
4. What does Mrs. Tsui do every morning?
5. Is she shouting at David this morning?
6. What time does her watch say?
7. What time does the bus leave?
8. What time does David's watch say?
9. Is it really half past seven?
10. What time is it?

Dialogue

Mrs. Tsui: David! It's time to get up.

David: It can't be time to get up yet.

Mrs. Tsui: It is. Hurry up! You'll be late for school.

David: What's the time?

Mrs. Tsui: It's nearly half past seven.

David: My watch says ten past.

Mrs. Tsui: It's slow. Hurry up! The bus goes at twenty to eight.

David: Are you sure it's half past seven?

Mrs. Tsui: Positive. I'll put the radio on.

Announcer: . . . . . and here is the seven o'clock news . . . . . .

David: It's only seven o'clock! Your watch is fast.

Mrs. Tsui: No it isn't. It's stopped! I forgot to wind it up last night.

David: I could have stayed in bed for another half hour!

Pronunciation Practice

Both these sounds are voiceless. Practise the first one. Put your tongue behind your bottom teeth and say /s/. Now put your tongue between your teeth and say /θ/.

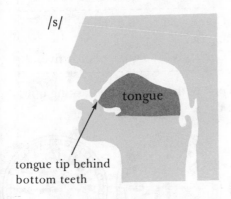

/s/

tongue tip behind
bottom teeth

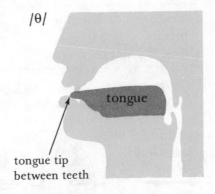

/θ/

tongue tip
between teeth

Here are some examples of /s/ and /θ/ at the beginning of words. Practise saying them aloud until you can say them clearly. Now work with your partner. Say one word and ask your partner if it belongs in column 1 or column 2. Go on until you have tested your partner with all the words.

/s/	/θ/
sink	think
sank	thank
sin	thin
sick	thick
some	thumb

Now here are some examples of the same sounds at the end of words. Do the same again.

/s/	/θ/
pass	path
use	youth
mouse	mouth
force	fourth
miss	myth

Language Practice 1

Here are some polite ways of asking for and giving the time:

What's the time, please? It's four o'clock.	Can you tell me the time, please? Certainly. It's quarter to two.
Would you tell me the time, please? Yes. It's half past eight.	Could you tell me the time, please? Certainly. It's quarter past five.

Now look at these clocks. Work with your partner asking questions and giving answers about the time.

The clock in the middle is right. The other clocks are wrong. Some of them are fast and some of them are slow.

Practise this conversation with your partner and then make up more conversations using the clocks and watches in the picture.

What's the right time?
It's five past three.
This clock says twenty past. It's fast.
Yes. It's fifteen minutes fast.

Language Practice 2

WHAT'S THE TIME?

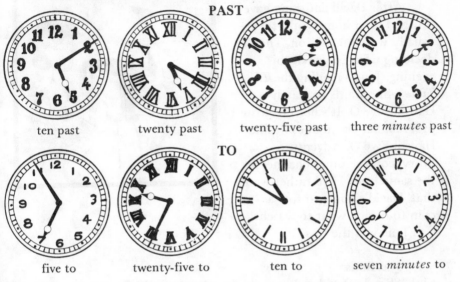

PAST

ten past   twenty past   twenty-five past   three *minutes* past

TO

five to   twenty-five to   ten to   seven *minutes* to

Do you remember the polite ways of asking the time? Look at these pictures and ask 'What time' politely. Here's an example for the first picture:

Can you tell me what time the bus goes, please?
Certainly. It goes at half past four.

goes 4.30/   leaves 6.05/   opens 8.30/
arrives 5.00   gets in 7.15   closes 7.45

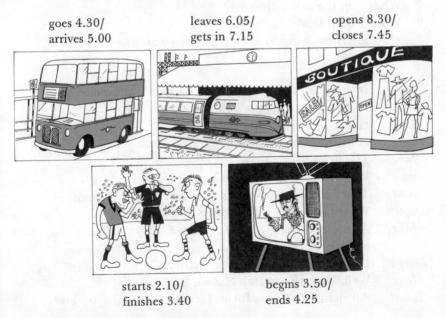

starts 2.10/   begins 3.50/
finishes 3.40   ends 4.25

9 What's On?

Situation

After David and Jane have finished their homework, they usually watch television. They're deciding what to watch this evening. Jane's reading the *TV Times*. She wants to watch Hawaii Five O. It's her favourite programme. David doesn't like Hawaii Five O. Adventure Story's on the other channel at the same time. He'd rather watch that. David's going to toss a coin to decide what to watch. Can Jane win the toss?

Questions

1 What do David and Jane do after they've finished their homework?
2 What are they doing now?
3 What's Jane reading?
4 What does she want to watch?
5 Is it her favourite programme?
6 Is it David's favourite programme?
7 What's on the other channel?
8 What would David rather watch?
9 How are they going to decide what to watch?

Dialogue

Jane: Is there anything worth watching on TV tonight?
David: I don't know. Where's the *TV Times*?
Jane: Here it is. What's the time?
David: It's nearly six o'clock.
Jane: The news is on at six.
David: What's on after the news?
Jane: There are some cartoons and then there's Adventure Story.
David: What time does Adventure Story start?
Jane: At quarter past six. But Hawaii Five O's on the other channel at the same time.
David: I'd like to watch Adventure story.
Jane: Well, I'd rather watch Hawaii Five O.
David: All right. We'll toss for it. Heads I win, tails you lose.

34

Intonation Practice

Can you whistle? Push your lips forward and try. Now, keep your lips in the same place and say /w/. Practise saying these question words: *What When Where Why Which*

In this unit we're going to talk about entertainment. Here are some sentences with /w/ sounds in them. Practise saying them aloud.

1 Is there anything worth watching on TV tonight?

2 Which channel's the programme on?

3 What time's the programme on?

4 I'd like to watch the news.

5 What would you like to watch?

6 When does the programme start?

Now, here are some pairs of words. Some of them start with a /w/ sound and some of them start with a vowel sound.

/w/	/vowel/
will	ill
win	in
wall	all
war	or
wear	air
wake	ache
wheel	eel
wages	ages
wonder	under

Language Practice 1

How many different conversations can you make from these sentences?

Is there anything worth	reading in the newspaper watching on TV listening to on the radio seeing at the cinema	today? this morning? this afternoon? this evening?

There's a good	article on page four. documentary on at nine o'clock. play on at half past three. film on at the Ocean Cinema.

What's it about?

It's about	High Island Reservoir. an Arctic explorer. a murder. a racing driver.

Now make some conversations of your own about these articles, programmes and films.

36

Language Practice 2

Do you know what the right time is?

nearly/almost   just/exactly   just after/just gone

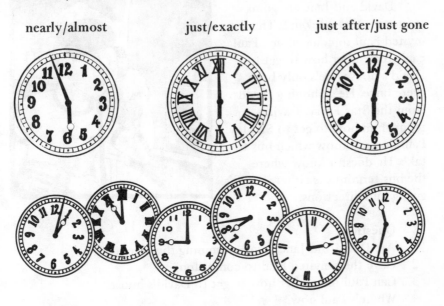

I'd like to watch Adventure Story. What would you like to watch?

The Mighty Thor (5.55 pm, RTV-2)

C TVB JADE

7.00 Superfriends
7.45 Cartoons
8.00 Izenborg
8.30 Candy Candy

E RTV 2

5.00 **Five O'Clock Club**
(Cartoons)
Johnny Cypher, Undersea Adventures Of Captain Nemo. Huckleberry Hound And The Mighty Hercules.
5.55 **Marvel Super Heroes**
IRON MAN
"DOUBLE DISASTER."
"ENTER HAPPY HOGAN."
"OF ICE AND MEN."
6.20 **Days Of Our Lives**
6.45 **News & Weather**
7.05 **Police Report & What's On**

C RTV 1

7.00 **Good Morning**
9.00 **Programme Summary**
9.03 **Mainly For Women**
9.30 **Cantonese Feature**
"MASTER SHAH AND SILVER MAID."
Starri

E TVB PEARL

9.00 **Cartoon Classics**
10.30 **Superfriends**
11.20 **Gumby Adventure**
11.45 **TV Funnies**
12.10 **The Alvin Show**
12.45 **Hector Heathcote**
1.10 **Abbott & Costello**
1.35 **Superman**
2.00 **A Very Merry Cricket**
A special Christmas cartoon for the whole family.

2.25 **The Liver Birds Christmas Special**
"IN EVERY STREET."
In the midst of their present wrapping and last-minute Christmas planning Carol and Sandra feel impelled to spread a little cheer among the less fortunate, but their good intentions cause more trouble than they intended.

3.05 **Bob Hope's Comedy Christmas Special**
Bob Hope hosts this spectacular

10 Lost

Situation

David and Jane are going swimming this weekend. They've invited Paul to come along. Paul can't remember how to get to David's house. He's only been there once. He's phoning David from the Star Ferry. David's telling him how to get to Stanley. Paul doesn't know which bus to take. He doesn't know where the bus terminus is either. David's giving him directions.

Questions

1 Are David and Jane going swimming this weekend?
2 Have they invited Paul to come along?
3 Can Paul remember how to get to David's house?
4 Where's Paul now?
5 What's he doing?
6 Does he know which bus to take?
7 Does he know where the bus terminus is?
8 What's David doing?

Dialogue

David: Hello? Hong Kong 939822.
Paul: Hello? Can I speak to David Tsui, please?
David: This is David speaking. Who's that?
Paul: David, this is Paul.
David: Hello, Paul. How are you?
Paul: Fine, thanks, but I can't remember how to get to your house.
David: Where are you now?
Paul: I'm phoning from the Star Ferry.
David: Hong Kong side or Kowloon side?
Paul: Hong Kong side. I don't know which bus to take.
David: Take a number six from the terminus. It goes to Stanley.
Paul: Where's the terminus?
David: Turn right outside the Star Ferry and walk past the new Post Office. The bus terminus is right in front of you.
Paul: Thanks very much. See you soon. Goodbye.

Pronunciation Practice

Here are two more vowel sounds. They are both long. When you say /ɜ/, smile a little. This will help you to make the right sound. When you say /ɔ/, push your lips forward.

/ɜ/	/ɔ/
work	walk
turn	torn
stir	store
fur	four
pearl	Paul
curl	call
burn	born
bird	bored

Practise all the words in column 1 first. Then practise all the words in column 2. Tell your partner to close his book. Say words from each column quickly. Ask him if they are number 1 sounds or number 2 sounds.

Read these sentences aloud. Each one has some /ɜ/ sounds and some /ɔ/ sounds. Say which words have /ɜ/ sounds and which have /ɔ/ sounds.

1 Mr. Tsui walks to work every day.
2 Paul likes birdwatching.
3 Mrs. Tsui burnt the rice last night.
4 Jane often dreams of having pearls and a fur coat.
5 David's bored with TV.
6 There are four people in the Tsui family.

Language Practice 1

HOW ARE YOU?

I'm fine.   I'm not too good.

I'm very well.   I'm not too bad.   I'm not very well.

Practise these conversations with your partner and then make up some more of your own. Ask your partner how he or she is and then ask about his family.

Q: How are you?
A: Fine, thanks. And you?
Q: I'm very well.
A: That's good.

Q: How are your parents?
A: Not too bad, thanks.

Q: How's your family?
A: They're all very well.

Q: How's your brother?
A: He's not too good.
Q: Oh dear. I'm sorry to hear that. What's wrong?
A: He's got a cold.

Q: How are you?
A: Not very well.
Q: That's a pity. What's the matter?
A: I've got the flu.

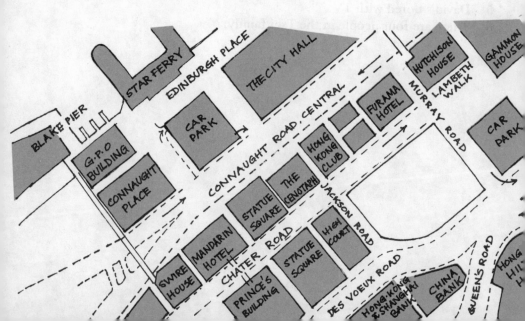

DIRECTIONS

turn right

turn left

walk past

walk along

walk up

walk down

in front of you

on your left

on your right

Here's a street map. Practise asking for and giving directions with your partner. Make questions and answers like this:

Q: Where's the bank?
A: Turn left outside the hotel and walk up the hill. The bank's on your left.

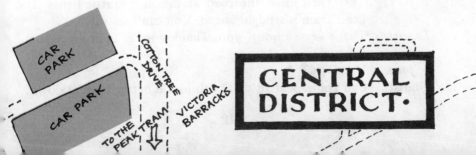

11 A Stranger to Town

Situation

Jane wears glasses. Yesterday she broke them so now she's on her way to the optician. She needs a new pair of glasses. A tourist has just stopped her. He wants to know the way to the Peak Tram. Jane's giving him directions. He's got a bad memory. He can't remember Jane's directions so he's asking her for a pencil. He wants to write everything down.

Questions

1 Does Jane wear glasses?
2 Is she wearing them today?
3 Why not?
4 Where's she going?
5 Who's just stopped her?
6 Why?
7 What's Jane doing?
8 Has the tourist got a good memory?
9 What's he asking Jane for?
10 Why?

Dialogue

Tourist: Excuse me.
Jane: Yes?
Tourist: Can you tell me the way to the Peak Tram, please?
Jane: Certainly. Go along Queen's Road . . .
Tourist: Along Queen's Road . . .
Jane: Yes, and turn right at the Hilton Hotel.
Tourist: Right at the Hilton.
Jane: Then go up Garden Road past the Cathedral.
Tourist: The Cathedral?
Jane: Yes. Then cross the road at the next traffic lights. The Peak Tram is straight ahead. You can't miss it.
Tourist: That's very kind of you. Thank you. Er . . . have you got a pencil?
Jane: Yes. Why?
Tourist: Can you repeat all that? I think I'd better write it down.

Read the tourist's first question aloud again. The first word, *can*, is not stressed. It's a weak word so the vowel sound is weak /ə/.

Tourist: Can you tell me the way to the Peak Tram, please?

There are three different pronunciations for the vowel sound in *can.*

1   Weak /ə/ in questions and statements. For example:

   Can you tell me the time, please?   I can tell you the time.
   /ə/   /ə/
   Can you show me the way, please?   I can show you the way.
   /ə/   /ə/
   Can you lend me a pencil, please?   I can lend you a pencil.
   /ə/   /ə/

2   Short /æ/ in positive answers. For example:

   Can you tell me the time, please?
   Yes, I can.
        /æ/
   Can you show me the way, please?
   Yes, I can.
        /æ/
   Can you lend me a pencil, please?
   Yes, I can.
        /æ/

3   Long /ɑ/ in negative answers and negative statements. For example:

   Can you tell me the time, please?
   I'm afraid I can't.
              /ɑ/
   Jane can't tell him the time.
        /ɑ/

   Can you show me the way, please?
   I'm afraid I can't.
              /ɑ/
   Jane can't show him the way.
        /ɑ/

43

Here are three different ways of asking *where?*:

Can you	direct me to the Peak Tram, please?
tell me	how to get to the Peak Tram, please?
	the way to the Peak Tram, please?

Now practise asking questions about these places. Notice that sometimes we use 'the' and sometimes we don't.

the	Star Ferry		Aberdeen		the nearest	police station
	City Hall		Lai Chi Kok			telephone
	Ocean Terminal		Waterloo Road			bank
	airport		Cheung Chau			bus-stop

Now, here's another street map. Practise asking for and giving directions with your partner. Here are some useful phrases:

Cross	the road at the next traffic lights.
	over at the pedestrian crossing.

Turn	right	at the	corner.
	left		crossroads.

It's	straight ahead.	
	opposite.	
	on the	right.
		left.

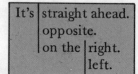

You can't miss it.

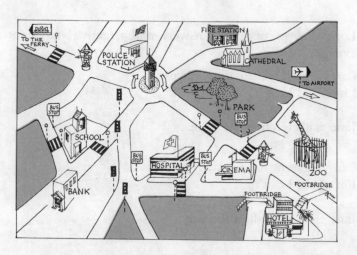

44

Language Practice 2

DO IT YOURSELF

Draw a street map of the area where you live. Put in your house, the roads near your house, bus-stops, tram-stops, shops and any other useful information. Then practise giving directions with your partner. Your partner will ask you:

Can you tell me how to get to your house?

He will point to the place on your map where he is standing. You must give him directions. From time to time, he will repeat the directions to make sure he's understood. Read the dialogue between Jane and the tourist once more before you start this exercise.

12 One of those Days

Dialogue

Situation

Mrs. Tsui's doing the washing. She's got a washing machine. It's old and doesn't work very well. The water's leaking. Mrs. Tsui's mopping it up as fast as she can but it's going through the floor. Jane's talking to the lady downstairs on the phone. The lady's angry because water's pouring through her ceiling. Now there's someone knocking at the door. What a day!

Questions

1 What's Mrs. Tsui doing?
2 Has she got a washing machine?
3 Is it new?
4 Does it work properly?
5 Is the water leaking?
6 Who's Jane talking to?
7 Why's the lady downstairs angry?
8 What's happening now?
9 Are Jane and Mrs. Tsui having a good day?

Dialogue

Jane: What are you doing?

Mrs. Tsui: I'm trying to mend the washing machine.

Jane: What's wrong with it?

Mrs. Tsui: There's something wrong with the hose. Look! The water's leaking all over the floor.

Jane: You'd better mop it up. It'll flood the flat downstairs.

Mrs. Tsui: I am mopping it up. Oh no!

Jane: What's the matter now?

Mrs. Tsui: The telephone's ringing.

Jane: I'll answer it.

Mrs. Tsui: Who is it?

Jane: It's the lady downstairs. She says water's pouring through her ceiling.

Mrs. Tsui: Tell her I'm mopping it up as fast as I can.

Jane: There's someone knocking at the door now.

Mrs. Tsui: Whoever it is, tell them I'm not at home!

/t/ /d/

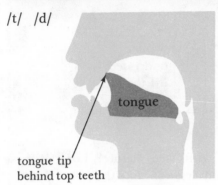

tongue

tongue tip
behind top teeth

/t/ is a voiceless sound and /d/ is a voiced sound. Put your tongue up behind your top teeth and practise saying:

/t/ /d/ /t/ /d/

/t/ /d/ /t/ /d/

It's easy to pronounce these sounds at the beginning of words. It's more difficult to pronounce them at the end of words. Here are some for you to try:

/t/	/d/
beat	bead
bet	bed
mat	mad
seat	seed
lit	lid
not	nod

Now look at these two pictures. Complete each sentence about the people in the pictures. Use one word for each sentence. The words for the first picture all end in /t/. The words for the second picture all end in /d/.

This man's very . . . . . .
He's wearing a . . . . . .
He's carrying a . . . . . .
He's got a black . . . . . .

This lady's very . . . . . .
She's got a handkerchief in her . .
She's listening to the . . . . . .
She's wishing she was . . . . . .

Language Practice 1

Here's a list of verbs all made with *get:*

get	out of bed
	ready for school
	into bed
	on the bus
	up

get	washed
	undressed
	off the bus
	dressed

Can you put the right verb with each picture? Look at these pictures of Jane's day and make conversations like this:

What's the time?   What's the time?
It's . . . . . .   It's . . . . . .
What's Jane doing?   Is Jane . . . . . .?
She's . . . . . .   Yes, she is./No, she isn't. She's . .

6.30 a.m.   7.00 a.m.   7.15 a.m.

7.20 a.m.   7.30 a.m.   8.00 a.m.

4.30 p.m.   9.00 p.m.   9.30 p.m.

Do you remember this?

>Jane: You'd better mop it up.
>
>Mrs. Tsui: I am mopping it up.

Notice that there is a stress mark on *am*. Usually we make the verb *be* very short in statements. We say *I'm* instead of *I am* and *he's* instead of *he is*. Mrs. Tsui says *I am* because she wants to emphasize her sentence. The main stress is on *am*.

Make short conversations with your partner using the prompts below. Here's an example:

She/hurry up   She'd better hurry up.

　/hurrying up   She is hurrying up.

Now you do the same and remember to put the strong stress on the verb.

1　You/turn it off.
　　/turning it off.
2　He/get up.
　　/getting up.
3　They/eat their dinner.
　　/eating their dinner.
4　She/do her homework.
　　/doing her homework.
5　You/close the window.
　　/closing the window.
6　You/wash your face.
　　/washing my face.
7　Jane and David/clear up the mess.
　　　/clearing up the mess.
8　She/do the washing up.
　　/doing the washing up.
9　He/clean the car.
　　/cleaning the car.
10　You/save some money for your holiday.
　　　/saving some money for my holiday.

13 The Philatelist

Dialogue

Situation

David enjoys sports very much. He plays football for the school team. Paul isn't very keen on sports. His main hobby's stamp collecting. Paul's sorting out his stamps. He's got quite a lot. He keeps them in his album. He got some new stamps yesterday. He's taking them off the envelopes. He's going to stick them in his stamp album.

Questions

1 Does David like sports?
2 Does Paul?
3 What does Paul do in his spare time?
4 What's Paul doing?
5 Has he got a lot of stamps?
6 Where does he keep them?
7 What did he do yesterday?
8 What's he doing with them?
9 What's he going to do next?

Dialogue

David: It's break-time. Come and play football.

Paul: No thanks. I'm sorting out my stamps.

David: Is stamp collecting your hobby?

Paul: Yes. I've got over four hundred stamps. Come and look.

David: Are these new ones?

Paul: Yes. I got them yesterday. I'm taking them off the envelopes.

David: What are you going to do with them then?

Paul: I'm going to mount them in my stamp album.

Daivd: Is stamp collecting an expensive hobby?

Paul: It can be, if you buy rare stamps.

David: Have you got any rare ones?

Paul: I had one, once.

David: What do you mean, you had one once? What happened to it?

Paul: I put it on a letter and posted it by mistake.

Do you remember this question?

David: What are you going to do with them then?

are and *to* both have very weak vowel sounds. Here's the question again with phonetic symbols showing the weak vowels:

What /ə/ you going /tə/ do with /ðəm/ then?

Practise asking this question with the stresses in the right places and the weak vowels.

Now here are some more questions. The question word always has a strong stress and the verb at the end of each question has a strong stress. *Are* and *to* are not stressed. They are weak sounds so be sure to pronounce them with the weak vowel /ə/.

1   What are you going to do?

2   Where are you going to go?

3   When are you going to come back?

4   Who are you going to meet?

5   Why are you going to buy it?

6   How are you going to carry it?

Language Practice 1

Let's go shopping. Practise this conversation with your partner.

Customer:	I'd like a loaf of bread, please.
Shopkeeper:	Yes, Sir. A small one or a large one?
Customer:	A small one, please.
Shopkeeper:	Here you are, Sir.

Now complete this conversation:

Customer:	. . . . . a can of peas, ...
Shopkeeper:	. . . . ., Madam . . . . . small . . . . . or . . . . . large . . . . .?
Customer:	. . . . . large . . . . ., please.
Shopkeeper:	Here . . . . ., Madam.

Practise this conversation with your partner:

Customer:	I'd like some socks, please.
Shopkeeper:	Yes, Madam. Cotton ones or nylon ones?
Customer:	Cotton ones, please.
Shopkeeper:	Here you are, Madam.

Now complete this conversation:

Customer:	. . . . . some gloves, ...
Shopkeeper:	. . . . ., Sir. Leather . . . . . or woollen . . . . .?
Customer:	Leather . . . . ., please.
Shopkeeper:	Here . . . . ., Sir.

Now make up some conversations of your own using these prompts. Be careful with *one* and *ones*.

1 an exercise book (lined or unlined?)
2 three pencils (hard or soft?)
3 some paper clips (metal or plastic?)
4 a dictionary (pocket size or full size?)
5 a ring binder (cardboard or vinyl?)

Language Practice 2

Something's going to happen. Make conversations like this:

Is the plane going to crash?
Yes, it is./No, it isn't.

Are the robbers going to escape?
Yes, they are./No, they aren't.

it/rain?

George/get better?

David/be late?

Mrs. Tsui/mop it up?

David and Jane/catch the bus?

number 13/win?

the Tsuis/have dinner?

David/play football?

14 Suicide Cat

Dialogue

Situation

David needs a new pair of football boots. He and Jane are in Central shopping. They're looking at a man. The man's standing on the roof of a very tall building. Jane thinks he's going to jump off. There's a fire engine coming. The siren's making a loud noise and the lights are flashing. Is it going to rescue the man?

Questions

1 What does David need?
2 Where are Jane and David?
3 What are they looking at?
4 Where's the man standing?
5 What does Jane think?
6 What's coming?
7 Is the siren sounding?
8 Are the lights flashing?
9 Why's the fire engine coming?

Dialogue

David: Look at that man up there!

Jane: Which man? Where?

David: The one standing on the roof of that building.

Jane: Do you think he's going to jump?

David: I don't know. Look! Here comes a fire engine.

Jane: One of the firemen's climbing up to the roof.

David: Yes, he's going to rescue the man.

Jane: Look! The man's crawling along the edge of the roof now.

David: What on earth's he going to do?

Jane: There's a cat right on the corner. He's going to rescue it!

David: He's giving the cat to the fireman. The fireman's going to bring it down the ladder.

Jane: The fire engine's driving away now. What's happened to the man on the roof?

David: He's still there. He's jumping up and down and shouting something.

Pronunciation Practice

These two sounds, /g/ and /k/ are made in the same way, but /g/ is voiced and /k/ is voiceless.

/g/ /k/

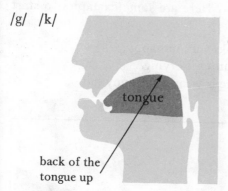

back of the tongue up

Practise saying these pairs of words:

/g/	/k/
goat	coat
gold	cold
gum	come
game	came
good	could

It isn't difficult to pronounce these sounds correctly when they come at the beginning of words. It's much harder when they come at the end. Practise these words with your partner and make sure the last sound in each word is clear:

/g/	/k/
back	bag
peck	peg
pick	pig
lock	log

Now try these sentences:

1 The doctor's carrying a big, black bag.
2 I can't get my key in the lock.
3 My back hurts and so does my leg.
4 Don't lick the gum off the envelope.
5 Could you take my book back to the library?

Language Practice 1

Look at this crowd of people. They're all wearing different clothes and they're all doing different things. How many sentences can you make about each person? Here are some examples to start you off:

1   The man wearing the hat looks very unhappy.
2   The lady standing by the counter is crying.
3   The man carrying the suitcase is wearing a funny hat.

Language Practice 2

What's happening?

What are all these people doing?

What are they going to do?

How many questions and answers can you make about this picture?

15 The Flu

Situation

Paul isn't at school today. He's at the doctor's surgery. Last night he felt ill. He still felt ill when he woke up this morning. His mother sent him to see the doctor. Paul's got a temperature. He's got a terrible pain in his stomach, too. The doctor's asking him a lot of questions. He's trying to find out what's wrong with his patient. He's asking Paul to describe how he feels. He wants to make him better.

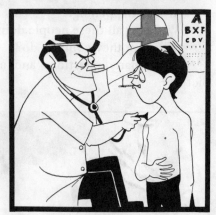

Questions

1 Is Paul at school today?
2 Where is he?
3 Did he feel ill last night?
4 Did he feel better this morning?
5 What did his mother do?
6 What's wrong with Paul?
7 What's the doctor asking him?
8 Why?

Dialogue

Doctor: Come in and sit down, Paul. Now, what's the trouble?
Paul: I've got a terrible pain in my stomach, Doctor.
Doctor: I see. When did it start?
Paul: It started yesterday. I didn't eat any supper.
Doctor: Have you got a temperature?
Paul: I think so. I feel very hot.
Doctor: Let's see. Yes. You've got quite a high temperature.
Paul: I've got an awful headache, too, and my throat hurts.
Doctor: Hmmmmmmmmmm. I think you've got the flu, Paul.
Paul: Is it serious?
Doctor: No, not at all, but you must stay in bed for three days and take this medicine.
Paul: How often must I take it?
Doctor: Three times a day after meals.
Paul: Thank you, Doctor. Goodbye.

Pronunciation Practice

It's very important to make your conversation flow smoothly. You can do this by joining the end of one word to the beginning of another. Let's look at some of the lines from the Dialogue and practise joining words into smooth sentences.

Paul: I've got a terrible pain in my stomach, Doctor.

Doctor: I see. When did it start?

Paul: Is it serious?

Doctor: No, not at all.

Paul: How often must I take it?

Doctor: Three times a day after meals.

When a word begins with a vowel, you can make the sentence smoother by joining the last consonant of the previous word to it. Look carefully at the joining marks on the sections from the dialogue above, and practise them again.

Here's an imaginary conversation between a doctor and his patient. Read it to yourself carefully and decide where to join words together. Make the joining marks with a pencil. Now practise the conversation with your partner. Speak as smoothly as you can.

Doctor: Come in and sit down. What's the trouble?
Patient: I've got a terrible pain in my arm, Doctor.
Doctor: I see. When did it start?
Patient: Three days ago.
Doctor: Take this medicine.
Patient: How often must I take it?
Doctor: Three times a day after meals.

Language Practice 1

Here are some different ways of talking about aches and pains:

I've got	stomach	ache
	back	
	ear	

but: I've got *a* headache.

He's got a	terrible	pain in his	arm.
	dreadful		leg.
	sharp		eye.
	dull		throat.

My hand	hurts.
wrist	
ankle	
elbow	

Now look at this picture. All the arrows point to different parts of this lady's body which hurt. Make as many questions and answers about her aches and pains as you can. Here are some example to help you:

Has she got stomach ache?
Yes, she has./No, she hasn't.

Has she got a pain in her arm?
Yes, she's got a terrible one.

Does her hand hurt?
Yes, it does./No, it doesn't.

60

Language Practice 2

TALKING ABOUT THE PAST

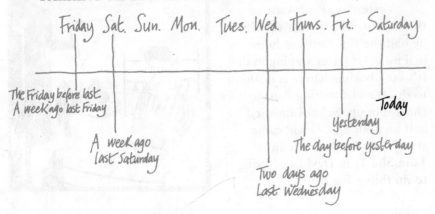

Now complete these sentences:

1 Today's Monday so it was Sunday . . . . . .
2 Today's Friday and I was ill on Wednesday. That was the . . . . .
before . . . . . .
3 Today's Thursday and my birthday was on Monday. That was
three . . . . . .
4 Today's Saturday and I played football last Saturday. That was
a . . . . . .
5 Today's Saturday and I played football a week ago. That was
. . . . . Saturday.

Now make up some sentences of your own. Say what you did
*yesterday, the day before yesterday, last Tuesday, a week ago, three
days ago.* Ask your partner what he or she did.

61

16 Visiting the Sick

Dialogue

Situation

Yesterday, Paul went to the doctor. The doctor told him he had the flu. Paul's at home in bed now. He hates staying in bed. It's very boring. There is nothing to do. David's visiting Paul to cheer him up. School finished half an hour ago. David came straight to Paul's house in Tsim Sha Tsui. David's offering to do things for Paul.

Questions

1 Is Paul back at school now?
2 Where did Paul go yesterday?
3 What did the doctor tell him?
4 What must Paul do?
5 How long must he stay in bed?
6 Does he like it?
7 Why not?
8 Who's visiting Paul?
9 What time of day is it?
10 Is David being helpful?

Dialogue

David: Hello. How are you feeling?
Paul: Awful.
David: Shall I open the window? It's a lovely day.
Paul: No thank you. I'm cold.
David: Shall I put the fire on?
Paul: Yes please, Will you turn it up high?
David: Are you sure? It's very hot in here.
Paul: I'm freezing. Will you get me another blanket, please?
David: Here you are. Shall I put it on the bed?
Paul: No. Put it round my shoulders, please.
David: ATCHOOOOOOOOOOOOO!!!!!
Paul: What's the matter?
David: Will you pass me one of your tissues, please?

Intonation Practice

When you are asking someone to do something for you, you should be very polite. One way of sounding polite is to say *please* at the end of your question, but this is not enough. You must make your voice sing a polite tune. Let's practise some polite requests. Make your voice rise at the end of each question:

Will you open the door for me, please?

Will you fetch me a pencil sharpener, please?

Will you give me some more rice, please?

Will you answer the phone for me, please?

You should also be polite when you are offering to do something for someone. Let's practise the intonation pattern for offering to do things. Again, your voice must rise at the end of each question:

Shall I open the door for you?

Shall I fetch you a pencil sharpener?

Shall I give you some more rice?

Shall I answer the phone for you?

Notice that you do not use *please* in offers.

Now try making some questions of your own. Ask you partner to do some things for you, then offer to do some things for him or her.

Language Practice 1

Do you remember this?

David: Will you pass me one of your tissues, please?

Notice the position of 'me'. It comes *after* the verb.

How many different sentences can you make from this table? The parts you can change are in boxes.

Will you	pass give hand throw	me him her them	one of your tissues, the soya sauce, the ball, her glasses,	please?

Now read this sentence again:

Paul: Will you get me another blanket, please?

Notice that *me* comes after the verb. You can say this sentence in another way:

Paul: Will you get another blanket for me, please?

Change these sentences using *for*.

1 Will you get me another cup of tea, please?
2 Will you fetch me some more paper, please?
3 Will you find me another pen, please?
4 Will you bring me a handkerchief, please?

Language Practice 2

Look at these pictures and then make two questions for each picture. First, make a *Will you* question, then make a *Shall* question. Here's an example:

Passenger: Will you carry my suitcase, please?
Porter: Shall I carry your suitcase for you, Madam?

Customer: bring/menu
Waiter:

Grandmother: close/window
Grandson:

Jane: find/glasses
David:

Mr. Tsui: fetch/coat
Mrs. Tsui:

Jane: get/*TV Times*
David:

David: pass/sugar
Mr. Tsui:

17 Life's Dull

Dialogue

Situation

It's Friday. David and Paul are in the school canteen. They've just finished lunch. David's fed up. He's talking to Paul about his life. He thinks his life's dull. He wants an exciting life. Paul's asking him questions about his daily routine.

Questions

1 What day of the week is it?
2 Where are David and Paul?
3 Have they had lunch yet?
4 Is David in a good mood?
5 How does he feel?
6 What's he talking about?
7 Does he think life's interesting?
8 What kind of life does he want?
9 What's Paul asking him about?

Dialogue

David: I'm bored.

Paul: Why?

David: Nothing interesting ever happens to me.

Paul: What do you mean?

David: Well, every day's exactly the same.

Paul: What do you do every day?

David: I get up, go to school, go home, do my homework and go to bed.

Paul: What do you do after your homework?

David: Sometimes I watch TV. Sometimes I read comics.

Paul: What do you do at the weekend?

David: Sometimes I go swimming. Sometimes I play football.

Paul: What do you want to do?

David: I want adventure, excitement, romance!

Pronunciation Practice

There are three different pronunciations for verbs in the present simple:

/z/	/s/	/ɪz/
goes	asks	washes

Here are some more for you to practise:

play — plays	stop — stops	watch — watches
read — reads	ask — asks	touch — touches
come — comes	sit — sits	pass — passes

Now read these sentences aloud and say which sound comes at the end of each verb:

1 David sometimes watches TV.
2 He gets up every day and goes to school.
3 He washes his face before he goes to school.
4 He catches the school bus near his house.
5 He always asks a lot of questions in class.

Look at these pictures. These are things Jane does every morning. Make one sentence for each picture. Start each sentence: 'Every morning Jane . . . . .'. Be careful with the sounds at the end of the verbs.

| 6.30 a.m. | 7.00 a.m. | 7.15 a.m. |
| 7.20 a.m. | 7.30 a.m. | 8.00 a.m. |

Language Practice 1

Do you remember this:

David: Nothing interesting ever happens to me.

You can use *ever* in a *negative* statement. Here are some examples:

Nobody ever helps me with my homework.
Nothing exciting *ever* happens to me.

Now complete these sentences using *nobody* ..... *ever* or *nothing* ..... *ever*.

1 . . . . goes to that restaurant.
2 . . . . . unusual . . . . . happens to us.
3 . . . . . nice . . . . . happens at the weekend.
4 . . . . plays with me.
5 . . . . . special . . . . . happens on my birthday.
6 . . . . answers my questions.

You can use *ever* in questions, too. Here are some examples:

Does David ever watch TV?
Yes. Sometimes.

Does David ever read comics?
Yes, Sometimes.

You can use *ever* in a question when you are not sure if the person does something or not. It would be silly to ask a question like: Do you ever get up in the morning? because everyone gets up in the morning.

Here are some ideas for you to ask your partner questions about:

cinema   theatre   chess   Enjoy Yourself Tonight
Cantonese Opera

Now try to think of some more *ever* questions you can ask your partner.

68

Language Practice 2

MORE TIME PHRASES

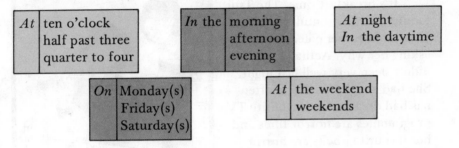

At	ten o'clock
	half past three
	quarter to four

In the	morning
	afternoon
	evening

At night
In the daytime

On	Monday(s)
	Friday(s)
	Saturday(s)

At	the weekend
	weekends

Practise these conversations:

1 What do you do on Saturday morning?
   I have a piano lesson at ten o'clock.
2 What do you do in the afternoon?
   Sometimes I go swimming. Sometimes I stay at home.
3 What do you do at the weekend?
   I help my Mum at home and sometimes I go to the cinema.
4 What do you do in the evening?
   I do my homework.
5 What do you do after your homework?
   I play games with my brother.

Now make up some more conversations of your own with your partner. Look at your school timetable and ask questions about that. Ask questions about the weekend and about things your partner does every day.

69

18 Nightmares

Situation

It's breakfast time. The Tsui family is sitting round the table. Jane looks rather pale. Mr. Tsui's asking her why. Actually, she didn't sleep very well last night. She had a nightmare. She often has bad dreams. Her favourite TV programmes are horror films and her favourite books are horror stories. Perhaps that's why she has bad dreams.

Questions

1 Is it lunch time?
2 Where's the Tsui family?
3 Does Jane look healthy this morning?
4 Did she sleep well last night?
5 Did she have pleasant dreams?
6 What kind of a dream did she have?
7 Does she often have bad dreams?
8 Why do you think she has bad dreams?

Dialogue

Mr. Tsui:	Morning, Jane. You look very pale this morning.
Jane:	Yes, Dad. I didn't sleep very well last night.
Mr. Tsui:	Oh? Why was that?
Jane:	I had a terrible nightmare. It was very frightening.
Mr. Tsui:	What did you dream about?
Jane:	The same thing as usual. Monsters.
Mr. Tsui:	The same thing as usual? Do you often dream about monsters, then?
Jane:	At least three times a week.
Mr. Tsui:	What do these monsters usually look like?
Jane:	They always have big claws and terrible eyes.
Mr. Tsui:	What do they usually do?
Jane:	They usually chase me.
Mr. Tsui:	Do they ever catch you?
Jane:	Never. I always get away.
Mr. Tsui:	Why do you dream about monsters so often?
Jane:	Probably because I read horror stories before I go to bed.

Pronunciation Practice

All these words come from the Dialogue. Some have an /l/ sound in them and some have an /r/ sound. Practise saying them slowly and make sure there is a clear difference between /l/ and /r/.

breakfast	looks	sleep	very
dream	favourite	horror films	horror stories
usually	claws	terrible	three
frightening			

Now do this exercise with your partner. Choose a sentence from the left hand column and read it to your partner. Ask him to give you the correct answer to the sentence.

1   Don't sit on the grass.   It's wet.
    Don't sit on the glass.   It's sharp.

2   That's a big cloud.   It's going to rain.
    That's a big crowd.   It's very noisy.

3   Where are the laces?   In your shoe.
    Where are the races?   At Happy Valley.

4   Turn on the light.   It's very dark in here.
    Turn right.   I can't. It's a one way street.

5   Put it on your wrist.   It's a very nice watch.
    Put it on your list.   I can't find my pencil.

Language Practice 1

Have a look at this time line. It shows when to use adverbs of frequency. *Frequency* means how often you do something.

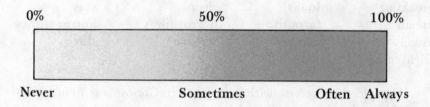

Usually is used for something you do at a particular time quite regularly. It's a word which you can use for routine happenings and actions.

Now practise these questions and short answers:

1   Do you always get up early?
    Yes, I do./No, not always.

2   Do you ever go to bed late?
    No, never./Sometimes.

3   Do you usually catch this bus?
    Yes, I do./No, not usually.

4   Do you often visit your grandmother?
    Yes, I do./No, not often.

Now make up some questions of your own. Ask your partner to give short answers.

Language Practice 2

Read these two conversations carefully:

1 Does Jane often have bad dreams?
Yes, she does.
Did she have one last night?
Yes, she did.

2 Do Mr. and Mrs. Tsui usually have breakfast with the children?
Yes, they do.
Did they have breakfast with them this morning?
Yes, they did.·

Notice that in the first conversation, *Jane* changes to *she* and *bad dreams* changes to *one*. Notice that in the second conversation, *Mr. and Mrs. Tsui* changes to *they* and *the children* changes to *them*.

Now complete these conversations.

1 Does Jane often read horror stories?
Yes, ...
. . . . read . . . . . last night?
Yes, ...

2 Does David ever read comics in the evening?
Yes, ...
. . . . read . . . . . yesterday evening?
Yes, ...

3 Do Mr. and Mrs. Tsui usually have dinner with the children?
No, ...
. . . . have dinner with . . . . . last night?
No, ...

4 Do David and Jane ever go to the cinema with their parents?
Yes, ... ·
. . . . go to the cinema with . . . . . last Saturday?
No, ...

19 A Bad Start

Dialogue

Situation

There's a public holiday on Monday. Today's Saturday. Mr. and Mrs. Tsui are taking the children to Macau for a long weekend. Mrs. Tsui always worries about things. Mr. Tsui thinks she worries too much. He's getting angry with his wife because she's asking so many questions. The hydrofoil's going to leave soon and Mrs. Tsui's worried about the tickets.

Questions

1 Is Monday a working day?
2 Is it Monday today?
3 Where are the Tsuis going?
4 How long for?
5 Does Mrs. Tsui worry about things?
6 Is she worried about anything now?
7 Is Mr. Tsui worried?
8 When's the hydrofoil going to leave?

Dialogue

Mrs. Tsui: Where are the children?
Mr. Tsui: They're over there, buying some sweets.
Mrs. Tsui: Have you got the bags?
Mr. Tsui: Yes, they're here. Don't worry so much.
Mrs. Tsui: Did you close all the windows?
Mr. Tsui: Yes, of course I did.
Mrs. Tsui: I didn't see you close them. When did you close them?
Mr. Tsui: Just before we left. Don't worry.
Mrs. Tsui: Did you lock the front door?
Mr. Tsui: Yes, of course I locked the front door.
Mrs. Tsui: Look! The gates are opening. Have you got the tickets?
Mr. Tsui: Yes, they're in my . . . . . oh dear.
Mrs. Tsui: Hurry up. We'll miss the hydrofoil.
Mr. Tsui: I put the tickets on the kitchen table before I closed the windows.
Mrs. Tsui: Didn't you put them back in your wallet?
Mr. Tsui: No, I didn't. They're still on the table!

Pronunciation Practice

When you're talking about things in the past, things that happened yesterday or last week, you use the *past simple tense*. All regular verbs end in *-ed* or *-ied* in the past simple. For example:

ache — ach*ed*
hurry — hurr*ied*

There are three different pronunciations for *ed* endings in the past simple. They are /t/, /d/ and /ɪd/. Here are some verbs to practise:

/t/	/d/	/ɪd/
lock — lock*ed*	close — clos*ed*	start — start*ed*
stop — stopp*ed*	move — mov*ed*	mend — mend*ed*
ask — ask*ed*	sail — sail*ed*	add — add*ed*
pass — pass*ed*	arrive — arriv*ed*	study — stud*ied*

Now read these sentences aloud and say which sound comes at the end of each verb:

1 Jane shivered because she was so cold.
2 She asked David to turn on the fire.
3 David turned it on and closed all the windows.
4 He passed his sister a warm sweater.
5 Jane started to feel better then.

Language Practice 1

Practise this section of the dialogue again with your partner:

Mrs. Tsui: Did you close all the windows?

Mr. Tsui: Yes, of course I did.

Mrs. Tsui: I didn't see you close them. When did you close them?

Mr. Tsui: Just before we left. Don't worry.

Notice where the stresses are. Make Mrs. Tsui sound worried and make Mr. Tsui sound angry. Now change the conversation using the prompts below, like this:

1   turn off all the taps

    Mrs. Tsui: Did you turn off all the taps?

    Mr. Tsui: Yes, of course I did.

    Mrs. Tsui: I didn't see you turn them off. When did you turn them off?

    Mr. Tsui: Just before we left. Don't worry.

2   turn off all the lights
3   put the tickets in your wallet
4   park the car in the garage
5   pack a clean shirt

Language Practice 2

Now it's Tuesday. Jane's back at school. She's telling Peter about her weekend in Macau.

Peter: Hello, Jane. Did you have a nice weekend?
Jane: Lovely, thank you.
Peter: Did you do anything special?
Jane: We went to Macau.
Peter: Did you have a good time?
Jane: Oh yes. We all enjoyed ourselves very much.

Jane uses *we* in her answers because she's talking about the whole family.

Let's look at Peter's first question again. There are several different ways he can ask about Jane's weekend:

Peter: Hello, Jane.

Did you have a	nice	weekend?
	good	
How was your weekend?		

Jane can answer in several different ways:

Jane:
Lovely, thank you.
Very good, thank you.
Very nice, thanks.

Now look at the ways Peter can change his second question:

Peter:

| Did you | do anything special? |
| | go anywhere interesting? |

Now make up some conversation of your own with your partner. Use as many different questions and answers as you can. Ask about your partner's weekend, last holiday, or birthday party. Perhaps you can think of some more things to ask about.

20 Homecoming

Situation

Luckily, Mr. Tsui managed to buy some more hydrofoil tickets. The whole family had a wonderful time in Macau. They caught the last hydrofoil back to Hong Kong on Monday. It's late Monday evening now and they've just arrived home. They're very tired but very happy. But there's something wrong. The front door's open . . . .

Questions

1 Did the Tsui family go to Macau?
2 Did Mr. Tsui manage to buy some more tickets?
3 Did the family have a good time?
4 Did they come back by ferry?
5 What's the time now?
6 Have the Tsuis arrived home yet?
7 How do they feel?
8 Is there anything wrong?

Dialogue

Mrs. Tsui: It was a lovely weekend. I enjoyed it very much.

Mr. Tsui: Yes. It was a good thing we managed to buy some more tickets, wasn't it?

Mrs. Tsui: We were lucky. I thought the hydrofoil would be full.

Mr. Tsui: Just a minute. The front door's open.

Mrs. Tsui: It can't be. You locked it before we left.

Mr. Tsui: Let's go in and have a look.

Mrs. Tsui: What a mess! Somebody's broken in.

Mr. Tsui: I'm afraid you're right. Look at these footprints. There were two of them.

Mrs. Tsui: They've searched everywhere.

Mr. Tsui: They've smashed a window and broken the lock on the door.

Mrs. Tsui: Have they stolen anything?

Mr. Tsui: Yes. They've taken the TV, David's transistor radio and your jewellery box.

Mrs. Tsui: Oh no! Whatever shall we do?

Mr. Tsui: Call the police at once.

Pronunciation Practice

Do you remember practising the weak vowel /ə/ in Unit Thirteen? Let's do it again. In the dialogue, Mrs. Tsui asks:

Have they stolen anything?

The vowel sound in *have* is weak /ə/. Now try question and answer. The vowel sound in *have* is weak /ə/ for the question form, but short /æ/ in the answer.

Have they stolen anything? /həv/ they stolen anything?
Yes, they have. Yes, they /hæv/.

Now make more questions and answers using these prompts. Be careful with the vowel sounds in *have*.

1   broken anything?
2   smashed any windows?
3   searched everywhere?
4   made a mess?
5   the TV?

Language Practice 1

This is what Mr. and Mrs. Tsui found when they got home.

Say what the thieves have done. Make as many sentences as you can like this:

They've	searched everywhere. smashed a window. broken the lock on the door.

Here are some words to help you:

knock over   break   tear   steal
take out   throw   open

Language Practice 2

Mr. Tsui phoned the police at once and a policeman came to make a report. Can you complete the conversation between Mr. Tsui and the policeman?

Policeman: What time . . . . . you . . . . . home, Sir?

  Mr. Tsui: About ten o'clock.

Policeman: How . . . . . the thieves . . . . . in?

  Mr. Tsui: They . . . . . a window and . . . . . the lock on the door.

Policeman: . . . . . they done much damage, Sir?

  Mr. Tsui: Yes. Look. They've . . . . . the curtains, ... everywhere and . . . . . a terrible mess.

Policeman: What . . . . . they stolen?

  Mr. Tsui: . . . . . taken the . . . . ., David's . . . . . and my wife's . . . . .

Policeman: I see, Sir. I'll make a report at once.

This is quite a short conversation. Perhaps you would like to try and make it longer. Look at the picture of the Tsui's flat and imagine you are Mr. Tsui showing the policeman around. Your partner is the policeman. He's asking you a lot of questions. When you've finished making up your own conversation, try to write it down.